VOICES OF EXPERIENCE

Practical Ideas to
Wrap Up the Year

Grades 4-8

VOICES OF EXPERIENCE

Practical Ideas to
Wrap Up the Year

Grades 4-8

CAREN CAMERON • KATHLEEN GREGORY
COLLEEN POLITANO • JOY PAQUIN

PORTAGE & MAIN PRESS

Portage and Main Press acknowledges the financial support of the Government of Canada through the Book Publishing Industry Development Program (BPIDP) for our publishing activities.

Printed and bound in Canada by Friesens

05 06 07 08 09 5 4 3 2 1

Library and Archives Canada Cataloguing in Publication

Practical ideas to wrap up the year : grades 4-8 / Caren Cameron ... [et al.]. (Voices of experience)

Includes bibliographical references.
ISBN 1-55379-033-2

1. Elementary school teaching.   I. Cameron, Caren, 1949-

II. Series: Voices of experience (Winnipeg, Man.)

LB1592.P73 2005   372.13   C2005-903159-X

PORTAGE & MAIN PRESS

100-318 McDermot Ave.
Winnipeg, MB Canada R3A 0A2
Email: books@portageandmainpress.com
Tel: 204-987-3500
Toll-free fax: 1-866-734-8477
Toll free: 1-800-667-9673

FOR JOY PAQUIN

In the summer of 2003, the four of us (Caren, Kathleen, Joy, and Colleen) worked together and planned the ideas for all the books in the Voices of Experience series. Shortly before the first two books went to press, Joy died suddenly. The ideas in this series reflect Joy's spirit.

Joy Paquin was a teacher's teacher. She was committed to making classrooms the best places for children and to sharing ideas with others. She was known for her enthusiasm, tireless dedication, and the fun she brought to teaching. Joy did more than teach children to read and write; she taught her students and her friends how to live a full and joyous life. Her  professional legacy –one of love, caring, humour, knowledge, and wisdom – will live on for thousands of children, parents, educators, and colleagues.

We dedicate this series to Joy, our dear friend, with love.

Caren, Kathleen, and Colleen

ACKNOWLEDGMENTS

Our thanks to the many new teachers we have met in our workshops, in our university classes, and in our schools. Your thoughtful questions have inspired us to design this series.

Kathleen, Caren, Colleen

Contents

Introduction

Who is this series for?

Voices of Experience is a series of six books – three for grades K-3, three for grades 4-8. Each book is full of practical ideas designed for new teachers, teachers new to a grade level, and teachers who want new ideas to reenergize their practice.

What's in the books?

We have compiled our best ideas and organized them into two sets of three books:

- Book 1: for the start of the year when teachers are just getting to know their students

- Book 2: for during the year when teachers need to get themselves and their students "fired up"

- Book 3: for the end of the year when teachers need to wrap things up

Each book is organized into four sections around the acronym ROAR.

R = ideas for building relationships

O = ideas for classroom organization

A = ideas for classroom assessment that support student learning

R = ideas that are reliable and ready to use tomorrow

"Create a new model of teacher to teacher support so that every teacher knows every other teacher's best ideas."

— Eric Jensen,
Brain-Based Learning

For each idea we provide a brief discussion and easy-to-follow steps. Many also include student examples and unique adaptations. In addition, we have included current information about the brain and how students learn.

We have also included a variety of ways to use this series of books to support professional development activities in different settings; for example, educators' book clubs; team and department meetings and staff meetings; in-service and pre-service workshops; and seminars with student teachers (see appendix A).

Final Note:

The single, most important message we want to leave you with is to listen to your own voice and the voices of your students. Adapt our ideas to fit for you, your students, and your school community.

INTRODUCTION TO RELATIONSHIPS

Establish trust and build relationships before anything else.
Then, place relationships above the rest.

■

Show students you care about them as people,
and let them see you as a person.

■

When relationships are established, students can
take risks and accept new challenges.

■

Emotion is a huge part of the classroom;
it often sets the stage for learning.

■

Relationships : First in the book, first in our classrooms.

In this chapter on relationships, we offer practical
ideas for you and your students to wrap up the
school year. Activities include ways to:

■ remember special events and times of the year

■ have a party to thank individuals for helping out in the class

■ work with peers in different classes

■ start a tradition where "leaving classes"
give a gift to the school

■ have peers recognize each other's strengths

Remember When:
keeping souvenirs of special events and times

> "Thinking and talking about experiences not only helps make sense of the past but also changes the likelihood of subsequent remembering."
>
> — Daniel Schacter, *The Seven Sins of Memory*

DISCUSSION

Stop and celebrate the milestone of nearing the end of the school year. We give our students time to talk about highlights of their year and to collect or make souvenirs as reminders of the special events and the time they spent together.

STEPS

1. Talk with students about souvenirs and why people keep them. We say, "Have you ever kept a souvenir from a ball game, a special event, or a place you've travelled to? Tell us what you kept and why you kept it. I'm going to ask you to think about some things we did this year and then I will ask you to find or make souvenirs to keep as reminders."

2. Work together as a class to make a list of the things students remember most about the year (see figure 1).

Remember when...

- we went to the Nature Centre
- you read us Breadwinner
- I remember the Ted Harrison pictures we painted (my Mom still has mine)
- James brought his goat
- our floor hockey team beat the teachers
- we all made those rockets in Science
- the class got to go and see the movie Holes after we read it
- we had math night
- we went on our ski trip to Mt. Washington
- we visited the museum
- we made our buddies a book

Figure 1. A list of events or times to remember

3. Discuss with students possible souvenirs they could find or make to fit with the specific times and events they wish to remember. Have them make a list of their ideas on chart paper (see figure 2).

4. Have students select 5-7 events or times they want to remember and a souvenir to represent each one.

5. Have students write a brief comment about what they want to remember most about each event by completing the phrase, "Remember when…" (see figure 3).

6. Decide on a container for the souvenirs and "remember when" comments such as a box, a bag, or a booklet. Our students make a booklet and leave the last page for autographs from their peers.

7. Set aside class time for students to select events, find or make souvenirs, and write their "remember when…" reflections.

8. Give students time to reminisce and share their "Remember when…" with classmates. We save the sharing time for the last couple of days of school and our students sign each other's booklets.

Remember When...	Souvenirs
1. Nature centre	my poster I made
2. ski trip	ski pass
3. buddies book	photocopy of cover
4. museum trip	I've got the brochure
5. floor hockey game	I'll draw a picture of Mr. Robinson in goal when they lost
6. paintings (Ted Harrison)	my painting
7. gymnastic routine	a picture of me doing the handspring

Black line master on p. 54

Figure 2. One student's list of "remember when…" and her souvenirs

Remember when...

we made books for our little buddies and Kyara loved hers

Figure 3. Student comments about what they want to remember

Special Thanks:
recognizing others for their support

"…simple acts of social caring can create positive affects for others."

— Storch, Maja, *Make Yourself Happy*

DISCUSSION

People need to know their efforts matter. We bring together individuals who have helped out or contributed in some way to our class during the year and have a party. This celebration is student-led, informal, and each guest is recognized and made to feel special.

STEPS

1. Talk with students about the importance of recognizing others who have helped the class during the year. We say, "So many people have helped us out during the year. We are going to have a party to let them know how much we appreciate what they have done for us."

2. Work together as a class to make a list of people to acknowledge and invite.

3. Decide on a time during school hours for the celebration. We typically use thirty to forty minutes before or after lunch

4. Record an agenda on a piece of chart paper and invite students to add ideas and suggest changes (see figure 4).

5. Make a list of snacks needed for the celebration and invite students to volunteer to bring one item (see figure 5).

6. Organize students into groups of three and have each group be responsible for writing an invitation to one guest, making

Thank You Party
Agenda

1. *welcome and seat guest*
2. *have snacks together*
3. *tell and listen to "thank you" stories*
4. *say goodbye and give gift*

Figure 4. A thank you party agenda

a small gift for their guest to take away, and telling a personal story about how the guest helped out. An example of a gift is a card that students have designed and signed.

7. Make copies of the invitation black line master on page 55, give one to each group, and have them complete and personalize it for their special guest (see figure 6).

8. Give students time in class to complete their invitations, to make a gift, and to prepare a thank you story.

9. On the day of the celebration, have students set places for their guests, welcome them into the classroom, and offer refreshments. We ask one student to be the host and welcome all the guests, go over the agenda, and invite students one at a time, to tell their personal "thank you" stories.

snack and supply list

Drinks (4 people)	cups and plates (3 people)
———————	———————
———————	———————
———————	
Napkins (2 people)	snacks (6 people)
———————	———————
———————	———————
	———————
	———————
	———————

Figure 5. Students volunteer to bring snacks and supplies.

To our special guest _____

You are invited to _____

When?_____

Where?_____

Why?_____

We are bringing snacks so please let us know if you can come.

From _____ Class _____

Black line master on p. 55

Figure 6. Outline of invitation for students to complete and personalize

Sign Up:
working with others for a change

"When we teach children how to make good choices and give them opportunities to do so, we give them feelings of capability."

—Martha Kaufeldt, *Begin with the Brain*

DISCUSSION

Expand friendships and increase motivation by giving students opportunities to work in different classrooms with different teachers and peers. Towards the end of the school year, we introduce the idea of "sign up" as one way to have our students self-select activities and work with a new group of peers who have similar interests.

STEPS

1. Find two or three colleagues who are interested in working together to offer activities for students from other classrooms.

2. Make a list of activities each teacher will offer (see figure 7). We offer options that are not too elaborate and do not create extra work at this time of year.

3. Select a day and time for "sign up." We choose a 40-minute period each week during the last month of school.

4. Make and post a chart for each classroom participating in the "sign up" that shows the activities in each room and the total number of students who can participate in each one (see figure 8).

<u>Ms. Gitzel's room</u>

Art and all types of arts and crafts activities (28)

<u>Mr. Belcher's room</u>

Card games (12)

Board games (12)

Computer games (12)

<u>Mrs. Bonfonti's room</u>

· CD headphone sets
· Create raps/songs
· Learn/create dance steps

(22)

<u>Mr. Hamilton's room</u>

Choice of sports equipment (gym/outside courts) (34)

Figure 7. Choices for "sign up" and number of spaces available

5. Ask students to choose one activity that interests them and have them "sign up" on the chart paper. If spaces are filled for one activity, students choose a different one.

6. On "sign up" day, ask students to go to the area or room to participate in the activity they've signed up for.

Figure 8. Students "sign up" for an activity that interests them

7. Ask students to return to their own classes to talk about their experiences with "sign up." Prompt students' thinking by asking questions such as, "Who did you get to work with?" "Did you meet anybody new?" "What did you like best?" "What suggestions do you have for next time?" "What would you go back and do again?"

8. Have students "sign up" for the following week.

Leave Your Mark:
creating a gift for the school

DISCUSSION

Year-end traditions help students gain a sense of closure. Our senior classes create or purchase something special to "leave their mark" before they change schools. This tradition gives students a sense of belonging and younger children look forward to taking part in the same practice when it's their turn.

STEPS

1. Talk with students about what traditions are and why they are important. We say, "This is your last year at this school and one tradition that this class might like to start is to make or buy something special to leave at the school. Years from now, people would know you were a student here because you've given something to leave your mark."

2. Ask students to meet in small groups to talk about possible ways for the class to "leave their mark."

3. Meet together as a whole class, and ask students for their suggestions. Make a list of these ideas on chart paper (see figure 9).

Ideas to "leave your mark"

- name tiles
- quilt
- make a picture collage
- mural in the hall
- buy a picture
- get a plaque for the school
- buy a book for the library and have our names in it – dedication
- get a bench for outside/playground
- banner in the gym
- plant a tree

other:

Figure 9. Class ideas for how to "leave your mark"

4. Have students discuss some of the pros and cons for each idea. We ask our students to think of possible locations in the school for permanent displays, and then to consider the costs, time, and skills involved.

5. Choose one idea that the class will use to "leave their mark." We have a class discussion and give our students a secret ballot to help make the decision.

6. Write a class letter to describe the idea and ask for approval from the school's administration. We ask one or two students to volunteer to present the letter to the principal, parent groups, and a school board member (see figure 10).

7. Give students time in class to work on the project. One year, our students designed individual name tiles that were put together in a display in the school hallway.

8. Set aside time at the end of the school year for a brief dedication ceremony. We take photos of this event to establish the importance of the tradition.

April 12

Dear *Administration*,

Ms. Gregory's class is leaving *Sangster School* this year and we would like to "leave our mark" by *creating name tiles*.

Some of our thinking includes:

• *Mr. King has tiles we can use for free*

• *it will look good in the hall by the gym*

• *our names will be in the school forever*

Please let us know if you will give us permission to "leave our mark" with the idea described above. If you have any questions or suggestions, please let us know.

Sincerely,
Ms. Gregory's Grade 7s

Figure 10. Class letter requesting permission to "leave our mark"

Keepers:
recognizing positive characteristics of peers

DISCUSSION

Peer recognition is powerful. We ask our students to give collective recognition to each other by identifying a positive personal characteristic for each person in the class. Students give each other a small object, or "keeper," as a reminder of the special characteristics they see in one another.

STEPS

1. Talk with students about the importance of recognizing the strengths of each person. We say, "We've all got strengths – and sometimes, we don't even know what they are until someone else tells us. We are going to take time and recognize each person in this classroom for a particular strength."

2. Post a list of positive personal characteristics (see figure 11). Discuss the meanings of the words with students and talk about examples of behaviours and actions that show these characteristics. Invite students to add other characteristics to the list.

Positive Personal Characteristics

- caring
- helpful
- honest (speak your mind)
- cooperative
- friendly
- kind
- compassionate
- generous
- fair (good sport)
- has good ideas
- true friend
- enthusiastic
- courageous
- likes to laugh (fun to be with)

Figure 11. List of positive personal characteristics

3. Decide on an object that will be given to each student as a "keeper." A favourite object we use is a small stone.

4. Give each student a class list. Have them select and record one characteristic for each person in the class.

5. Collect each student's class list with characteristics. We look through the lists and find the characteristic for each student that is repeated most often.

Figure 12. One student's keeper

6. Record the characteristic that identifies each student's overall strength on an object or "keeper." We have student volunteers print these words on rocks with permanent markers.

7. Have a special ceremony where the "keepers" are handed out to each person in the class. Our students hand out their rocks to each other at our year-end celebration.

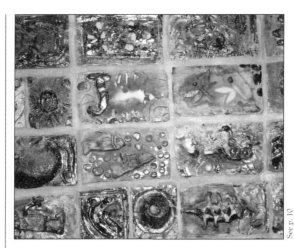

Figure 13. Students made tiles to "leave their mark."

See p. 10

Figure 14. A student takes a souvenir out of her special "remember when" box.

See p. 4

Figure 15. Students give their teacher/librarian an invitation to "special thanks" party.

See p. 6

INTRODUCTION TO ORGANIZATION

Organize in ways that maximize learning.

■

Take time to set up routines and procedures with students;
it saves in the long run.

■

Organize in ways that allow all students to make independent
use of materials, spaces, and routines in the classroom.

■

Organization is more than having a neat and tidy classroom.
Organization is about creating a positive,
safe, and orderly environment.

■

The best way to organize is the way that works
best for you and your students.

In this chapter on organization, we offer practical ideas
for you and your students to wrap up the school year.
Activities include ways to:

- give students independent contract work

- use roles to read nonfiction material

- ask questions to challenge students' thinking

- give time for students to take a break

- spend a day working on one subject area

Contract Time:
making choices and working independently

> "Making choices
> is like lifting weights.
> The more frequently
> students choose from
> a group of options
> the thicker their
> 'responsibility muscles'
> become."
>
> — Thomas Armstrong,
> *Multiple Intelligences
> in the Classroom.*

DISCUSSION

Give students opportunities to show they are responsible learners. One way to do this is to have students work on contracts that require them to make choices, organize their own schedule, and complete tasks on time.

STEPS

1. Talk to students about what contracts are and how they can be used in classrooms. For example, we say, "A contract is an agreement between two people. A contract in this class is between you, the students, and me, the teacher. I will give you some work to complete and you'll decide which tasks you plan to do, what you'll work on first and how long you will spend on each activity."

2. Give students a sample contract. We photocopy and distribute the black line master on page 56 and discuss each task (see figure 16). The contract activities we ask students to do are ones they've worked on before and do not require our direct instruction.

3. Have each student select their tasks and sign a contract. For students who need to be challenged, or who require smaller chunks of work or more time, we adjust the number of tasks we ask students to complete. To meet the needs of all of our students, contracts need to be realistic and challenging, not frustrating.

4. Make copies of the rubric black line master on page 57 and give one to each student. Discuss the criteria and the three levels of quality in the rubric (see figure 17).

5. Set aside a block of time each day for "contract time." We typically use an hour or more each day and we monitor class progress by stopping and asking, "What are you working on now?" "How long do you think it'll take to finish this part?" "Do you have something for me to check or mark?"

6. Have students hand in their completed contracts and mark them using the contract rubic. For each criterion we shade in one level of performance on the rubric that most closely matches the work students have done.

7. Talk with students about what worked, what did not work, and what changes could be made for the next contract.

8. Have students set up a new contract for the following week.

Contract for _poetry_
(subject)

I, the undersigned, agree to complete _6_ tasks selected below by _June 15_.

WRITE ✓	USE COMPUTER ✓	WRITE ☐
Choose a special place and write an acrostic poem.	Write 5 similes and illustrate using clip art.	Use the biopoem pattern and write about yourself.
READ ALOUD ✓	**RESEARCH & WRITE ☐**	**ILLUSTRATE ✓**
Select a poem, practice reading it, and read it aloud to 3 people.	Choose a poet. Learn some facts and write a found poem to show what you have learned.	Find a poem you like. Copy it and illustrate it.
WRITE ✓	**INTERPRET ☐**	**MEMORIZE ☐**
Write a poem that a 3 year-old might enjoy.	Read the poem and answer the questions on the sheet.	Choose a poem you like. Memorize it and recite it to someone.
YOUR CHOICE ✓	**YOUR CHOICE ☐**	**YOUR CHOICE ☐**
Read Shel Silverstein's book of poetry.		

Signed _____John_____   _____Mrs. Stone_____
              (student)   (teacher)

Black line master on p. 56

Figure 16. A contract a student has agreed to and signed*

*Adapted from *Multiple Intelligences in the Classroom*

Criteria for Contract Work	Pro	Semi-Pro	Rookie
1. Use independent time wisely	you used your time well every day	most days you made good use of time	you needed several reminders about use of time
2. Complete agreed upon contract	you've completed all work	you've completed all but one piece	you've completed some parts and more work is required
3. Do quality work	all work is of high quality with no corrections or additions needed	most work is done well with only 1 or 2 changes needed	some work is done well and other parts require a significant number of corrections or changes

Black line master on p. 57

Figure 17. Rubric for marking contracts

Reading Roles:
reading nonfiction material effectively

" ..if students are able to verbalize and 'flesh out' ideas with other students, or work together on group projects, the thought becomes anchored in understanding."

— Carla Hannaford,
Smart Moves

DISCUSSION

Having a purpose for reading helps the brain focus. Towards the end of the school year, when our students' attention tends to wander and they need a change in routine, we introduce an activity called "reading roles." This organizational structure lets students take a single focus when they are reading nonfiction material and requires them to be accountable to a group of peers.

STEPS*

1. Explain the purpose and steps of "reading roles" to students. For example, "I'm going to teach you an activity called 'reading roles.' You are going to work in small groups and each person will read for a different purpose. Rather than answering questions when you are finished reading, you are going to meet and talk about what you've learned."

2. Photocopy the black line master on page 58 and give each student a copy (see figure 18).

3. Discuss each role with students. For example, for the role of illustrator, we talk about including specific and accurate details and trying to capture the key ideas of what is being said, rather than spending time making an attractive picture.

4. Organize students into groups of three, and assign each student a role.

5. Select a short piece of nonfiction text and read it aloud to students.

6. Give students a few minutes to complete their role assignment by recording information on their sheets.

7. Have each group meet to show and talk about what they learned in their roles. We find that five minutes is often enough time to share information.

8. Assign a piece of text for students to read independently to practice nonfiction reading roles. We remind our students, before they begin reading, to decide on their role so they can focus on one aspect and report to their peers.

9. Discuss "reading roles" with the class by asking, "What worked?" "How did your role help you stay focused?" "What role did you like the best?" "What new roles would be interesting to add?"

*Adapted from *Literature Circles: Voice and Choice in Book Clubs and Reading Groups*

ADAPTATION

When students are watching a video, listening to a guest presenter, or observing a science lab, have them take on a specific role to help them focus.

Reading Roles for Nonfiction

Name _____

ILLUSTRATOR: Your job is to sketch and label pictures and diagrams to show key facts.

Date
_____
Topic
_____

QUESTIONER: Your job is to write 2-3 questions to ask or talk about in your group.

-
-
-

Date
_____
Topic
_____

FACT FINDER: Your job is to record and tell 3-5 key facts you learned or confirmed.

-
-
-

Date
_____
Topic
_____

Black line master on p. 58

Figure 18. Nonfiction reading roles

Hands Down:
asking everyone in the class to respond

DISCUSSION

Four words that improve instruction are "talk less; ask more."
In an activity called "hands down," we ask questions that challenge our students to think about their understandings, thoughts, and beliefs. We give them time to think and talk with each other before answering and we expect every student in the class to have a response ready.

STEPS*

1. Talk with students about how questions can really make us think. For example, we say, "I'm going to ask you some questions that can be answered with a variety of ideas and from different points of view. I will give you time to think and talk with someone before I ask you to give a response. This activity is called 'hands down' because I don't want people putting up their hands. I expect everyone to be ready with a response."

2. Pose a question that is not related to any particular subject area and have students practice "hands down" (see figure 19).

Sample Questions

Why do you think some schools are requiring students to wear uniforms? What's your opinion?

What do you think about keeping wild animals in captivity?

Some people say large SUVs use up too much energy and should not be driven. What do you say?

Why do you think people are telling us to conserve our water? What are your ideas?

Figure 19. Questions for practicing "hands down"

3. Give students time on their own to think, and then have them turn to a partner and talk about their thoughts. We ask students to pair up with someone nearby rather than getting up and moving across the room.

4. Bring everyone in the class together and ask any student to respond to the question. We then we first use "hands down," our students need reminders not to put up their hands or call out answers.

5. Tell students that if they don't have a response at this time, they can say "I don't have an answer right now." To keep students thinking about the question, and not "let them off the hook," we make it clear that we will come back to them again and ask for their thoughts.

6. After a response, invite other students to add on to what classmates say, disagree, give support, give a different response, or suggest more examples.

7. Keep the pace of "hands down" brisk by asking a variety of individuals to respond and then posing a new question.

8. Debrief with students by asking, "How did it feel to be expected to answer each question?" "What question really made you think?" "What other questions would be interesting to ask?"

9. When students are familiar with using "hands down," pose questions that are related to specific subject areas (see figure 20).

*Adapted from *Assessment for Learning*

ADAPTATION

Instead of having students meet with a partner to talk about their thinking, give students 2-3 minutes to write or sketch their thoughts on a piece of paper.

Hands Down Questions
Citizenship

1. All would-be citizens of our country are required to take a test. What do you think people coming to our country should know before they become Canadian citizens?

2. Why do you think people in our province can get their driver's licence at 16 years of age but have to wait until they are 18 years old to vote?

3. Would-be citizens of Canada need to swear (or affirm) that they will be faithful and loyal to Her Majesty, Queen Elizabeth II. What are your thoughts about this?

Figure 20. Subject-related questions for "hands down"

Brain Breaks:
taking time to refocus and reenergize learners

"…'energizers' or quick little wake up activities increase energy levels, improve storage and recall of information, and help learners feel good."

— Eric Jensen,
Learning With the Body in Mind

DISCUSSION

Mind and body work together. Make time each day to have brief brain breaks to help students become more productive learners. Two effective ways we invite students to take breaks and be leaders are with "group patterns" and "chain reaction".

IDEA #1 GROUP PATTERNS

STEPS

1. Tell students they are going to learn a new "brain break" called "group patterns".

2. Demonstrate a pattern of physical movements for students to follow. Have them watch and join in (see figure 21).

3. Tell students that they will work in groups to create their own set of actions to teach the class.

4. Organize students into groups of three or four.

5. Give time for each group to come up with their own patterns and actions.

Slap knees twice

Cross hands over chest and tap shoulders twice

Slap knees twice

Cross hands over chest and tap shoulders twice

Slap knees once and cross one hand over and tap opposite shoulder

Slap knees once and cross the other hand over and tap the opposite shoulder

Slap knees three times

Repeat the pattern

Figure 21. Teacher demonstration of "group patterns"

6. Stop during the day for "brain breaks." Each time you stop, ask a different group to teach the group pattern they created. We make time for brain breaks two or three times during the day.

IDEA #2 CHAIN REACTION

STEPS

1. Tell students that they are going to learn a new "brain break," called "chain reaction."

2. Ask a volunteer to step outside the class.

3. Have students arrange themselves in the classroom so they can see every other person. We ask our students to stand in a circle around the perimeter of the class.

4. Choose one student in the circle to lead the class in simple hand and arm movements.

5. Ask all students to follow the leader. When the leader changes actions, everyone in the circle follows along. As the goal is to make it impossible to tell who the leader is, followers are careful not to look directly at the leader.

6. Have the volunteer return to the classroom, watch the activity, and guess who is leading the group.

7. A new volunteer steps outside the class and the activity is repeated.

Subject Marathon:
spending chunks of time on one subject

DISCUSSION

Maximize student engagement by changing the organization of the day. We reorganize one day of our timetable so the class can spend the day working on one subject. The novelty of "subject marathon" can motivate learners and the single focus allows students to consolidate their learning.

STEPS

1. Tell students that their timetable will be changed so they can spend more time focusing on one subject. We say, "We usually work on a subject for about an hour every day. For the last month of school, I've changed our timetable. Once a week we are going to have a 'subject marathon,' where we spend the day on one subject only. You won't have to clean up and move on to different topics and you can have time to actually finish something you start."

2. Decide on one subject area for "subject marathon" and determine the skills or process for students to review. We begin with social studies and ask our students to work through the research process.

Key components of social studies subject marathon	Suggested Times
· Decide on research question(s)	
· Find and read sources	
· Collect facts and make notes	
· Summarize answers to research question(s)	
· Share research findings	
· Select another question and repeat	

Figure 22. Key components of a social studies "subject marathon"

3. Set up a schedule for "subject marathon." We try to set aside one full day, and if that is not possible, we use a morning or an afternoon.

4. Record on a piece of chart paper the key skills or components to be completed for "subject marathon." Review each component with students and suggest the amount of time each might take to complete (see figure 22).

5. Ask students to begin working on key components and monitor their progress. We give students a choice of working with a partner or on their own, and provide an outline for them to organize their research (see figure 23).

6. Have the class stop at different times during the day to check and see what individuals are working on, how far along they are, and how much more time they need.

7. Bring the class together towards the end of the "subject marathon" and have each person or pair share their research findings. We have students share with a partner or in small groups rather than have them present in front of the whole class.

8. Debrief "subject marathon" with students by asking, "How did this work?" "Did you find you had enough time?" "How many people completed all the components and started again?"

ADAPTATION

Another curriculum area for "subject marathon" is the writing process (see figure 24).

Name(s): _____ *attach your notes
Research Outline
Research Question(s)
•
•
•
Sources I used
•
•
•
Summary

Black line master on p. 59

Figure 23. Research outline for "subject marathon"

Key components of a "writing marathon"	
Ideas:	choose something to write about
Partner:	talk about what you plan to write about
Draft:	write your ideas down quickly on paper
Partner:	read your draft to a partner and get advice
Revise:	make changes
Proofread:	check for spelling and punctuation
Publish:	decide how to publish and make it perfect
Share:	find someone to read your work to
Start again:	choose a new idea

Figure 24. Key components of a "writing marathon"

See p. 18

Figure 25. Students meet to show and talk about what they learned in their "reading roles."

See p. 22

Figure 26. One group follows the teacher's actions for "group patterns."

INTRODUCTION TO ASSESSMENT

Assessment is information about learning: what is working, what is not, what happens next.

■

Our first goal for assessment practice is to support student learning not simply measure it.

■

Descriptive feedback is what contributes most dramatically to learning.

■

The more students are involved in their own assessment, the more they learn.

■

Students are more likely to achieve goals they set for themselves than ones set for them.

In this chapter on assessment, we offer practical ideas for you and your students to wrap up the school year. Activities include ways to:

■ have students develop their own criteria

■ mark for the purpose of supporting student learning

■ use students' ideas to create a rubric

■ create a year-end portfolio

■ celebrate each student's progress and growth

Peer Feedback:
listing criteria and asking peers for feedback

DISCUSSION

Achievement increases when learners are involved in their own assessment. Towards the end of the year, many of our students have internalized "what counts" and they are ready to take a lead role in monitoring their learning and improving their work. We offer one effective routine that requires students to list their own criteria for an assignment and to collect specific feedback from peers.

STEPS

1. Remind students about the importance of setting criteria and receiving feedback. We say "When you know what counts before you start an assignment, it helps you focus on the important parts. I'm going to ask you to list your own criteria for an assignment and ask your classmates for feedback."

2. Give students an assignment to complete. We select something that students are familiar with and still needs more practice or review, such as making a presentation.

3. Make copies of black line master on page 60 and give one to each student. Ask students to record key areas they want to receive feedback on (see figure 27).

4. Demonstrate how to complete the "peer feedback" sheet. We suggest that our students list a minimum of three criteria and receive feedback from at least three peers.

5. Give students time in class to work on the assignment and to request feedback from peers.

6. Invite students to use the feedback they receive from peers to make improvements. We find that our students give feedback in language that others in their age group can relate to and use.

7. Debrief by asking "How did deciding on the criteria help you in this assignment?" "How did the peer feedback help you?"

My criteria for _my presentation on Nunavut_
<ul><li>loud enough</li><li>using charts and pictures</li><li>I was organized</li><li>it was interesting to listen to</li></ul>

Peer Feedback	Peer Feedback
To: Katie	To: Katie
From: Kris J.	From: Megan
<ul><li>I could hear it all</li><li>hold the chart still</li></ul>	<ul><li>I liked your pictures but you</li><li>didn't tell where they lived</li></ul>
Peer Feedback	Peer Feedback
To: _____	To: _____
From: _____	From: _____
<ul><li></li><li></li></ul>	<ul><li></li><li></li></ul>

Black line master on p. 60

Figure 27. Student criteria for presentation, and "peer feedback"

Figure 28. A students gives a presentation and peers give feedback.

Comments Only:
marking to increase student achievement

"When classroom teachers give (descriptive) feedback they create a climate of success."

— Candace Pert,
Molecules of Emotion

DISCUSSION

Different purposes for marking require different techniques. When the purpose for marking is measurement and accountability, we use evaluative feedback in the form of numbers, percentages, or scores. When the purpose is to support learning and increase achievement, we use descriptive feedback that identifies strengths and areas that need improvement. We use "comments only" as one technique to support our students' learning.

STEPS*

1. Explain to students that there are different purposes and different ways to mark their work. We say, "Sometimes I will mark your work by giving you a score out of 10, or a grade. This type of marking is for measuring how you are doing. The problem is that these symbols or numbers do not tell your brain what you did well or how you can improve. So at other times, I will *mark* your work using "comments only" to let you know your strengths, weaknesses, and the next thing you need to do to improve."

2. Show students an example of "comments only" marking (see figure 29).

3. Give students an assignment and the criteria. We use assignments that we have already developed criteria for, such as reader response (see figure 30).

4. Use "comments only" to mark student work.

5. Return work to the students and give them time in class to use the comments to improve their work.

6. Give students frequent opportunities to receive "comments only" marking. We give students two or three opportunities to complete reader responses and receive "comments only" before we ask them to select one of their responses to be evaluated with a number or score.

7. Meet as a class and ask students to discuss the types of comments they need to hear in order to help them improve their work.

*Adapted from Assessment for Learning

Comments Only Marking

For _reader response_

Student _Betty Tate_

2 **things you've done well:**

· you followed the format

· told me about the main character

1 **area that needs improvement:**

· tell more of your ideas about the book
  (what you think)

DO **this for your next step:**

· write how you felt when the character left home

Date: _April 25_ Class: _Grade 6_

Figure 29. Reader response marked using "comments only" technique

Criteria for Reader Response	Details
follow the format	• record page numbers you read • put the date on the top • record the title of the book and author if you have just started a new book
Give 2-3 key ideas from the story	• tell about characters and what they did • say where and when it is happening • tell what happens
Make personal connections to the story	• ask questions • make a prediction • tell how you feel or react • say what you liked or didn't like
Write so others can read it	• write neatly • use complete sentences • check your spelling and capitals

Figure 30. Criteria for reader response

Class-Constructed Rubrics:
using student ideas and language to increase understanding

DISCUSSION

Students understand what they create. Take time to involve learners in the construction of rubrics so they can understand the language and focus on the learning. We find class-constructed rubrics help students identify their strengths and recognize what they need to do to improve.

STEPS

1. Explain to students what rubrics are and how they can be useful. We say, "You've seen and used rubrics before and now we are going to create one together. A rubric has a list of criteria and descriptions of levels of quality. When we work as a class to make a rubic, everyone has a clearer picture of what is expected and you can use it to find out your strengths and what you need to work on."

2. Draw a blank grid for a rubric on a piece of chart paper (see figure 31). We purposely develop three levels of quality. With more than three levels it becomes difficult to write descriptions that make clear distinctions between levels. Also, we title each level on the rubric with non-judgmental words that

Criteria for	There	Almost there	Getting there

Figure 31. Blank rubric showing three levels of quality

Black line master on p. 61

focus on progress and growth. We do not use numbers, as our students end up focusing on the score and not on the learning.

3. Decide on a specific activity or performance for a class-constructed rubric. We choose activities that our students will be doing more than once before the school year ends, such as free-choice reading, reader response journals, working with a partner, problem-solving, or group work.

4. Record criteria for an activity such as group work on the left hand side of the rubric (see figure 32).

5. Work with students to develop descriptions for each criterion. We begin at the *there* or "top" level of the rubric and prompt students' thinking by posing questions such as, "What does it look like when you are working well together?" "Do you work well together the whole time?" "Does everyone in the group work well, or just some people?"

6. Listen to students' descriptions, and "pull out" their useful words and phrases. Record these on the rubric. We remind students that the most important purpose of class-constructed rubrics is to support learning, so the language needs to relate to progress and growth. We use phrases such as "starting to…," "needs some help in…," "needs more time to….," rather than language that relates to failure such as "weak," "poor," "lousy," or "inadequate."

7. Continue working together as a class to develop a description for each criterion at each level of the rubric (see figure 32).

8. Try out the rubric when students work in groups and then revise it together. We have learned not to expect perfection the first time students develop a rubric.

9. Give students frequent opportunities to self-assess their performance in relation to their class-constructed rubric.

Criteria for Group Work	There	Almost There	Getting There
Get Along	Everyone got along (almost always).	Most people got along most of the time.	Some people worked OK together and others didn't.
Share Ideas	Everyone in our group gave ideas.	Most people had ideas – some more than others.	A few people gave ideas.
Listen to Others	Our group listened carefully to each other. We tried not to interrupt.	Most of us were trying to listen to everyone so we could hear their ideas.	We need to get better at listening to the group and not talking to just one person.
Finish the Job	We completed all the work on time and did it thoroughly.	We got the job done - may have rushed one part.	We need more time to finish.
Use Voices That Don't Bother Others	We consistently used quiet voices.	We were reasonably quiet most of the time.	We tried to use quiet voices. Sometimes we needed reminders.

Figure 32. Class-constructed rubric for group work

Wrap-Up Portfolios:
selecting and reflecting on work samples

"A person's own record of accomplishments … strongly influences current and future output."

— Mel Levine M.D., *The Myth of Laziness*

DISCUSSION

Portfolios have the power to focus students' attention on their learning efforts and accomplishments. We have students recap their learning and growth by assembling "wrap-up portfolios" at the end of the year.

STEPS*

1. Explain to students the purpose of a "wrap-up portfolio." We say, "I want you to look back on the things you've done in this school year and select specific samples of your work. You can choose work samples, photos, peer and self-assessments, or anything else that shows your accomplishments. You're going to put this evidence of your learning together in a 'wrap up portfolio' to show others."

2. Give students a table of contents that shows the types of work samples (evidence) they are to include in their "wrap-up portfolios" (see figure 33).

3. Give students time during the last month of school to select work samples to fit with the table of contents. We ask our students to choose 5-7 categories from the contents list.

4. Have students complete a written reflection on each work sample by answering three questions (see figure 34):

   • What did you do?

   • What do you want others to notice?

   • What did you learn?

5. Have students decide on a holder for their "wrap-up portfolio."

Our students use a variety of things including boxes, cardboard folders, pocket portfolios, and large envelopes.

6. Set aside time in class for students to show their "wrap-up portfolios" to others (see figure 35).

*Adapted from *Knowing What Counts: Conferencing and Reporting*

Figure 35. Student shows her portfolio.

Table of Contents	Name _____
Select samples of your work that show the following:	Your sample
☐ All Time Best	
☐ Unique Approach	
☐ Took a Chance	
☐ Greatest Improvement	
☐ Accuracy	
☐ Enjoyment	
☐ Lose it!	
☐ Expert	
☐ Other:	

Figure 33. Table of contents for "wrap-up" portfolios

Took a Chance

• What did you do?

I made a charcoal drawing.

• What do you want others to notice?

It really looks like me.

• What did you learn?

I can show shadows by shading.

Figure 34. A student's completed reflection

Black line master on p. 62

Portfolio Showing:
celebrating learning
with others

"Celebrating student learning is the most fundamental, most motivating and most powerful affirmation for the learning community."

— Judy Carr and Douglas Harris, *Succeeding with Standards*

DISCUSSION

Establish a year-end celebration where students show and talk about their learning to others. We have learned that "portfolio showings" are powerful and possible when we keep them brief and positive and they highlight growth and progress over the year. Our audiences include a variety of individuals such as family members, coaches, custodians, friends, and former teachers.

STEPS*

1. Have students organize a collection of work samples into "wrap-up portfolios" (see p. 34).

2. Schedule one class period in the library towards the end of the school year for "portfolio showing." We've learned to keep "portfolio showings" separate from report cards to keep the emphasis on celebration rather than on evaluation of learning.

3. Let students know they will be inviting guests to the "portfolio showing."

4. Work together with students to make a list of potential guests to invite (see figure 36). We ask our students to think of people who are older than they are and who care about their learning. We invite additional guests to make sure each student has someone to show his/her work to.

5. Make copies of the black line master on page 63 and give one to each student. Have students complete and personalize their invitation for one or more guests on the list (see figure 37).

List of Guests

· moms and dads

· stepmoms

· Mr. Powell, my soccer coach (and other coaches)

· Mrs. Campsall, our TA

· Ken, our daytime custodian, and Rose, who cleans our room

· Lisa, our secretary (and Sue)

· my grade 1 teacher at Sangster (and other teachers we've had)

· my aunt

· our principal

other:

Figure 36. List of guests for year-end "portfolio showing"

6. Give time in class for students to practice showing and talking about their portfolios with a peer.

7. Develop an agenda for the "portfolio showing" with students (see figure 38).

8. Have students show and talk about their work with their invited guest(s) on the day of the "portfolio showing." We bring cookies and drinks to add to the atmosphere of celebration.

9. Remind students to ask their guests to complete a comment card before leaving (see figure 39).

10. Debrief with students by asking them to respond orally, or in writing, to two questions: What are your thoughts about the "portfolio showing"? What is your advice?

*Adapted from *Knowing What Counts: Conferencing and Reporting*

Portfolio Showing

                                                    May 31

Dear Mrs. Newton,
        (guest)

On May 28 our class will be sharing our
      (date)   year-end portfolios.

On this day please come to the library
at 1:00 - 2:00 .   (place)
   (time)
Three highlights of my learning this year
that I will show and talk about are

1. the myth I wrote

2. my geometry test

3. my report on mummies

Please let me know if you can come so I
can tell my teacher.

Yours truly,
Deanna

Figure 37. Completed invitation for "portfolio showing"

Agenda for Portfolio Showing

Purpose:
to celebrate students' progress and growth

1. welcome guests and introduce them

2. show and talk about your portfolio

3. ask guests to complete response cards

4. go to the refreshment area together

5. visit the computer lab (if time allows)

Figure 38. Agenda for portfolio showing

**Portfolio Showing
Comment Card**

Celebrating student learning is motivating.
Please offer two compliments to the learner
about what you saw today.

To Deanna

1. You are a fine writer. I think your myth
   should be published.

2. Well done on your test.

signed Mrs. Newton

date May 28

Figure 39. Comment card completed by a guest

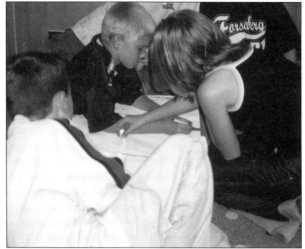

See p. 44

Figure 40. One group collects key ideas and creates visuals in preparation for "teach it."

See p. 36

Figure 41. Family members are guests at year-end portfolio showing.

INTRODUCTION TO RELIABLES

Reliables are ideas that can be depended on to
keep students active and engaged.

■

Reliables are activities that work with a wide range of learners.

■

Reliables offer students choices to show what they know.

■

Reliables let students personalize their learning.

■

With reliables, students know what to anticipate, and
they can say: "Oh, we know how to do this!"

In this chapter on reliables we offer practical
ideas for you and your students to wrap up the school year.
Activities include ways to:

- have students ask and answer questions

- summarize information in different ways

- have students do the teaching

- retell favourite books

- review in unique and active ways

Questions and Clues:
learning where to "look" for the answer

DISCUSSION

Help students gain confidence in their ability to answer and ask questions. In "questions and clues," teachers and students alternate asking and answering questions and students learn exactly where to look for the answer.

STEPS

1. Tell students they are going to learn to ask and answer different types of questions.

2. Record three types of questions on a piece of chart paper: one literal (on the line), one inferential (between the lines), and one where students have to connect to their own experiences (beyond the lines). We start with questions about something that most students are familiar with such as *Goldilocks and the Three Bears* (see figure 42).

3. Ask students one question at a time and have them tell how they knew the answer. For example, "It said there were three bears in the title of the story."

4. Work with the class to develop a visual clue for each type of question to remind students where they need to "look" for answers (see figure 43).

Types of Questions

On the line
"How many bears are in the story?"

Between the lines
"How did baby bear feel when he found someone in his bed?"

Beyond the lines
"Should Goldilocks be punished? If so, how?"

Figure 42. Types of questions to remind students where to look for answers

5. Make an overhead transparency of a paragraph and show it to the class. Ask students to read the paragraph silently.

6. Ask students an "on-the-line" question. We make sure that we tell students the type of question we are asking and refer them to visual clues on the chart.

7. Ask a volunteer to answer the question and then underline on the overhead where he or she found the answer.

8. Alternate roles and have students ask the teacher an on-the-line question. We remind students to identify the type of question before they ask it.

9. Give students practice asking and answering on-the-line questions before they ask between-the-lines or beyond-the-lines questions.

10. Teach students how to ask and answer the other two types of questions by repeating the steps. Over time, our students recognize that each type of question requires them to go to a different place to find the answer.

11. Once students are familiar with all three types of questions, use "questions and clues" for any piece of text.

Figure 43. Visual clues for types of questions developed by the class

ADAPTATION

When students are familiar with asking the three types of questions, we assign a point value. For example, an on-the-line question is worth 1 point, a between-the-lines question is worth 2 points, and a beyond-the-lines question is worth 3 points. We ask students to make up questions to total 20 points. For example, a student could choose to write six beyond-the-line questions and one between-the-line question, to total 20 points.

Summary Frames:
giving students a guide to organize ideas

"Stronger memories are formed each time the information is expressed... even when the review is very brief."

— Candace Pert,
Molecules of Emotion

DISCUSSION

Summarizing is one of the most useful skills to teach students. When students summarize, they are more likely to recall the information. We offer two practical ways to help students find the key ideas and record them succinctly.

IDEA #1: DID YOU KNOW?

STEPS

1. Tell students they are going to learn a new way to summarize information.

2. Record the "summary frame" on a piece of chart paper (see figure 44).

3. Select a brief piece of informational text. We choose news or magazine articles that our students will find interesting.

4. Work with students to complete the first section, called, "You probably know…" before reading the text.

5. Read the text aloud to students. Ask them to tell any new information they learned about the topic.

Did You Know?

Topic: *Bethany Hamilton*

You probably know:

- *she was bitten by a shark*
- *she was surfing*
- *she lost her arm*

But did you know:

- *she is not wearing a fake arm*
- *she is a semipro surfer*
- *she is better than ever with one arm*
- *she's written a book called Soul Surfer*
- *she says her faith and family helped her*

by – *the class*

Figure 44. Example of one "summary frame" using ideas from students

---

Record these ideas in the second section, called, "But did you know…?" on the "summary frame."

6. Give students time to practice using the idea, "Did you know?" on their own or with a partner.

IDEA #2 THREE-WORD WEB

1. Tell students they are going to learn another way to summarize information.

2. Record the "summary frame" for a three-word web on chart paper (see figure 45).

3. Select a short piece of text, read it aloud to students and ask them to listen for key ideas.

4. Identify one key idea from the text and record it inside one circle. Ask student volunteers for two other key ideas and record these in the other circles

5. Show students how to create the web of related information and details around one key idea. Ask volunteers to give their ideas that relate to the other two circles. Record this information on the web (see figure 46).

6. Give students opportunities to practice working on their own or with a partner to create their own "three-word webs" so that it becomes a reliable way for them to summarize information.

Three-word web

Topic:_____ name:_____

Black line master on p. 65

Figure 45. Example of a "three-word web"

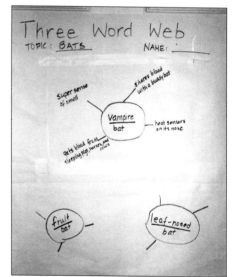

Figure 46. Partially ompleted "three-word web" about bats

Teach It:
having students do the teaching to review

DISCUSSION

Engage students at the end of the year by asking them to teach others a specific concept or topic. We divide key ideas of a unit into small, manageable chunks and ask students to teach the information to peers as a way of review.

STEPS

1. Tell students that they are going to work with others to teach their classmates about a topic. We say "You've seen me teach all year long. You know how it's done, what works best, and what doesn't work at all. Now it's your turn to select part of a unit and teach it to others."

2. Decide on a unit and divide it up into small chunks or topics. For example, a science unit on weather could include the study of specific terms (see figure 47).

3. Record specific tasks for each group to complete for the part of the unit that they will be teaching (see figure 48).

4. Discuss each of the tasks with students and show examples where necessary.

Weather Words

- earthquakes
- hurricane
- precipitation
- air mass
- humidity
- atmosphere
- thermometer
- global warming
- clouds – cirrus, cumulus, stratus
- tsunamis
- tornado
- barometer
- El Niño
- evaporation
- air pressure
- fronts

Figure 47. Weather words from a science unit

5. Organize students into groups of three and have each group select one part to teach. To make sure all of the weather terms are reviewed, we record each word on a separate piece of paper and have one student from each group select two or three.

6. Give students time in class to complete the tasks for their part of the unit.

7. Set aside class time for students to teach one another. We set a time limit of 30 minutes and groups present to as many other groups as they can within that time frame.

8. Have students give each group of "teachers" specific feedback (see figure 49).

Teach-It Tasks

1. *present* 5-7 key points

2. *create* 1-2 visuals or a handout

3. *ask and answer* 3-5 questions.

Figure 48. Three tasks for "teach it"

Teach-It Feedback

To: _____
          (teach-it group)

From: _____
              (peer)

I learned:

_____
_____
_____

I liked:

_____
_____
_____

Black line master on p. 66

Figure 49. Peer-feedback form for "teach it"

Storytellers:
retelling our favourite books

"Stories provide a schema or a script for us to tag or anchor information into our memories."

— Karen Markowitz,
The Great Memory Book

DISCUSSION

Retelling is a powerful way to take a second look at favourite books. We ask students to think of some of their "old favourites" that they read over the school year. Each student chooses a book and plans a retelling using real objects or symbols. These storytellers bring a sense of closure to the school year.

STEPS

1. Talk with students about the variety of books they have read this year.

2. Work with the class to make a list of their favourite books (see figure 50).

3. Tell students that they are going to select one favourite and present a retelling of the main parts of the story. Let them know the unique part of the retelling is that they will use real objects or symbols to make it interesting and fun.

4. Model a retelling of a favourite book. We retell a book we have read to the class such as *Zlata's Diary*. We follow a retelling frame and show each object or

---

Our Favourite Books

Where the Red Fern Grows	*Pearl Harbour*
	Mummies
Tuck Everlasting	*Midnight Fox*
Breadwinner	*Eric Wilson's Mystery*
Bridge to Terabithia	*Gordon Korman's Island trilogy*
Tuk (the bear)	
Kindest Cut	*Hatchet*
Young Child in Prison Camp	*Manon Rheaume*
The Story of the Titanic	*Zlata's Diary*

Figure 50. Class list of favourite books (fiction and nonfiction)

symbol and talk about how it connects to an event in the story (see figure 51).

5. Demonstrate ways to engage an audience. For example, we pull out one object at a time and keep others hidden in a bag to create suspense.

6. Ask students to select a favourite book that they want to retell.

7. Photocopy the black line master on page 67 and give a copy of the retelling frame to each student to use as a guide.

8. Give students time in class to fill in the frame and find or make objects or symbols.

9. Set aside time for students to retell their "old favourites" during the last week of school. We use approximately 15 minutes per day to have "storytellers" present their retellings.

Retelling Frame

My favourite is _Zlata's Diary_

5 – 7 KEY IDEAS	OBJECTS or SYMBOLS
Zlata writes in her diary	a pencil
There is war all around her in Sarajevo	drawing of a war scene
she has her 12th birthday and there is no electricity	a birthday candle
The whole city is on fire	a picture of fire
Her mother keeps listening to the radio to see if they can escape from the city	a picture of a radio
Zlata had to leave her home and country and friends to live in peace	draw a peace sign

Black line master on p. 67

Figure 51. Completed retelling frame for teacher demonstration

60-Second Flashbacks:
choosing quick ways to review

"…seemingly lost information can be recovered by hints or clues that remind us of how we initially encoded the experience."

— Daniel Schacter,
Seven Sins of Memory

DISCUSSION

End the year with a positive feeling about learning. A useful and active way to have students think about what they have studied during the year is to use "60-second flashbacks." Students give a brief, creative presentation on a character, creature, country, or concept as a way of review.

STEPS*

1. Tell students they are going to learn how to review by doing an activity called "60-second flashback." We say, "To help recall key ideas we have learned this year, you are going to choose different ways to show what you remember about a character, creature, country, or concept we've studied."

2. Make and post a list of some of the characters, creatures, countries, and concepts studied during the year. Ask students to suggest other ideas and add these to the list (see figure 52).

We have studied:	
Julius Caesar	Scorpions
King Tut	Rome
Galileo	Egypt
Halley	Mesopotamia
Nefertiti	Pyramids
Brian (in Hatchet)	Volcanoes
Stanley (in Holes)	Ratio
Silverwing (bat's name in the trilogy)	Round up
	Estimation
Salmon	Perspective in art
Jellyfish	Colour wheel
Kinds of whales	

Figure 52. Some characters, creatures, countries, or concepts the class has studied

3. Talk with students about possible ways to present a "60-second flashback." Record them on a piece of chart paper (see figure 53).

4. Have students choose an idea to review and a way to present their "60-second flashback." We give students the choice of working on their own, with a partner, or with a small group.

5. Ask volunteers to demonstrate what a "60-second flashback" can look like so everyone can see what they are expected to do in a very short period of time.

6. Make a schedule and invite students to sign up.

7. Give time for students to present their "60-second flashbacks." We start each day with five presentations.

8. Talk with students about their favourite parts of the "60-second flashbacks" and how these presentations helped them remember ideas they learned during the year.

*Adapted from *Inspiring Active Learning*

Choose one way to present a 60-second flashback

Mime: show the idea with actions and no words

Puppet: have a puppet explain key ideas

Model: make a model to show the idea

Skit: use words and actions to present the idea

Be the character: find something to wear or say to give clues about the character

Collage: cut out words, pictures, and designs to show main points

Poster: draw and design a poster to show key information

Figure 53. Possible ways to present a "60-second flashback"

Appendix A
professional development

USING THIS BOOK WITH ADULT LEARNERS

The ideas in this book can be used to support professional development activities in different settings; for example, educator's book clubs; team and department meetings and staff meetings; and in-service and pre-service workshops.

Consider the following possibilities:

BRAIN BITS

This idea works well as a way to introduce the book at a staff meeting (where only two or three books might be available).

1. Make a copy of the Brain Bits black line master (page 68) for each participant.

2. Organize the participants into small groups (three or four per group), and have each member in the group do the following:

    (a) Choose a "brain bit."

    (b) Read aloud the quotation to the others in the group.

    (c) Discuss how he/she can relate the "brain bit" to his/her students and experiences in the classroom.

    (d) Invite group members to make comments or ask questions.

3. Have the groups continue until each person in the group has had a turn.

4. Bring all the groups together, show them copies of Voices of Experience, and invite a couple of volunteers to read the books and try some of the ideas with their students.

5. At the next staff meeting, ask the volunteers to discuss what ideas they tried and what they learned.

Jigsaw

Jigsaw is a quick way to introduce the book to the participants. This idea works well at staff meetings or pre-service teacher seminars (when there are large numbers of participants).

1. Divide participants into groups of four. Assign a different section of the book (Relationships, Organization, Assessment, Reliables) to each person in the group.

2. Ask each person to read his/her assigned section and to be prepared to summarize and retell a favourite activity.

3. Each person, in the group of four, takes a turn to talk about his/her section.

4. Invite participants to select one idea that they will try out with their students. Ask each person to come to the next meeting with student samples and stories to share.

Book Club

This idea works when at least two people are interested in the book.

1. Invite colleagues to form a book club (two or more people make a club).

2. Agree on a time and place for the first meeting.

3. At the meeting, decide how to work with the book. A couple of suggestions: (a) each member reads a different section of the book and selects one activity to try with students, or (b) the group comes to an agreement on one section of the book to read and one idea to have everyone try out before the book club meets again.

4. At the end of the meeting, set a time to get together again. Agree to bring back student samples and stories about what worked, what did not work, and what adaptations were made.

5. Invite participants to record their next steps on a planning sheet (see page 69).

INDEPENDENT STUDY

This idea works well for teachers who choose to work on their own – especially those who are new to the profession and those who are working at a new grade level.

1. Read the book to get an overall sense of its contents (20 ideas for a 20-minute read).

2. Select one or two ideas to try out with students.

3. Use the record sheet to keep track of the idea you have tried, how well it worked, and what idea to try next (see Recording Sheet, page 70).

TAKE ACTION

This idea works well at meetings and workshops.

1. Invite adult learners to try out activities for themselves during staff meetings and workshops. Here are some possibilities:

■ "Remember When" (page 4)

Take time at a year-end staff meeting to remind each other of some of the "highlights" that have taken place during the year.

■ "Keepers" (page 12)

Have staff identify positive personal characteristics of colleagues and make "keepers" for each other at the end of the year.

■ "Reading Roles" (page 18)

Have participants in a workshop or staff meeting use roles to read informational material. Roles such as questioner and fact-finder can help teachers share a reading task with colleagues and concentrate on one aspect of the information.

■ "Brain Breaks" (page 22)

Give participants time for brain breaks during meetings or workshops.

Appendix B
black line masters

Remember When...	Souvenirs
1.	
2.	
3.	
4.	
5.	
6.	
7.	

Figure 2. (page 5)

To our special guest

You are invited to _____

When? _____

Where? _____

Why? _____

We are bringing snacks so please let us know if you can come.

From _____

Class _____

Figure 6. (page 7)

Contract for _____
(subject)

I, the undersigned, agree to complete _____ tasks selected below by _____.

WRITE ☐	USE COMPUTER ☐	WRITE ☐
Choose a special place and write an acrostic poem.	Write 5 similes and illustrate using clip art.	Use the biopoem pattern and write about yourself.
READ ALOUD ☐	**RESEARCH & WRITE** ☐	**ILLUSTRATE** ☐
Select a poem, practice reading it, and read it aloud to 3 people.	Choose a poet. Learn some facts and write a found poem to show what you have learned.	Find a poem you like. Copy it and illustrate it.
WRITE ☐	**INTERPRET** ☐	**MEMORIZE** ☐
Write a poem that a 3 year-old might enjoy.	Read the poem and answer the questions on the sheet.	Choose a poem you like. Memorize it and recite it to someone.
YOUR CHOICE ☐	**YOUR CHOICE** ☐	**YOUR CHOICE** ☐
Read Shel Silverstein's book of poetry.		

Signed _____   _____
(student)   *(teacher)*

Figure 16. (page 17)

Criteria for Contract Work	Pro	Semi-Pro	Rookie
1. Use independent time wisely	you used your time well every day	most days you made good use of time	you needed several reminders about use of time
2. Complete agreed upon contract	you've completed all work	you've completed all but one piece	you've completed some parts and more work is required
3. Do quality work	all work is of high quality with no corrections or additions needed	most work is done well with only 1 or 2 changes needed	some work is done well and other parts require a significant number of corrections or changes

Figure 17. (page 17)

Reading Roles for Nonfiction

Name _____

ILLUSTRATOR: Your job is to sketch and label pictures and diagrams to show key facts.

Date

_____

Topic

_____

QUESTIONER: Your job is to write 2-3 questions to ask or talk about in your group.

-
-
-

Date

_____

Topic

_____

FACT FINDER: Your job is to record and tell 3-5 key facts you learned or confirmed.

-
-
-

Date

_____

Topic

_____

Figure 18. (page 19)

Name(s): _____ *attach your notes

Research Outline

Research Question(s)

-
-
-

Sources I used

-
-
-

Summary

Figure 23. (page 25)

My criteria for _____

- _____
- _____
- _____
- _____

Peer Feedback	Peer Feedback
To: _____	To: _____
From: _____	From: _____
• _____	• _____
• _____	• _____
Peer Feedback	Peer Feedback
To: _____	To: _____
From: _____	From: _____
• _____	• _____
• _____	• _____

Figure 27. (page 29)

Criteria for _____	There	Almost there	Getting there

Figure 31. (page 32)

All Time Best	Unique Approach
• What did you do? • What do you want others to notice? • What did you learn?	• What did you do? • What do you want others to notice? • What did you learn?
Took a Chance	**Greatest Improvement**
• What did you do? • What do you want others to notice? • What did you learn?	• What did you do? • What do you want others to notice? • What did you learn?
Accuracy	**Enjoyment**
• What did you do? • What do you want others to notice? • What did you learn?	• What did you do? • What do you want others to notice? • What did you learn?
Lose It!	**Expert**
• What did you do? • What do you want others to notice? • What did you learn?	• What did you do? • What do you want others to notice? • What did you learn?

Figure 34. (page 35)

Portfolio Showing

Dear _____ ,
(guest)

_____
(date)

On _____ our class will be sharing our
(date)
year-end portfolios. On this day please

come to _____ at_____ .
(place) _(time)_

Three highlights of my learning this year
that I will show and talk about are

1.

2.

3.

Please let me know if you can come so I
can tell my teacher.

Yours truly,

_____

Figure 37. (page 37)

Portfolio Showing Comment Card

Celebrating student learning is motivating.
Please offer two compliments to the learner.

To _____

1.

2.

signed _____ date _____

Figure 39. (page 37)

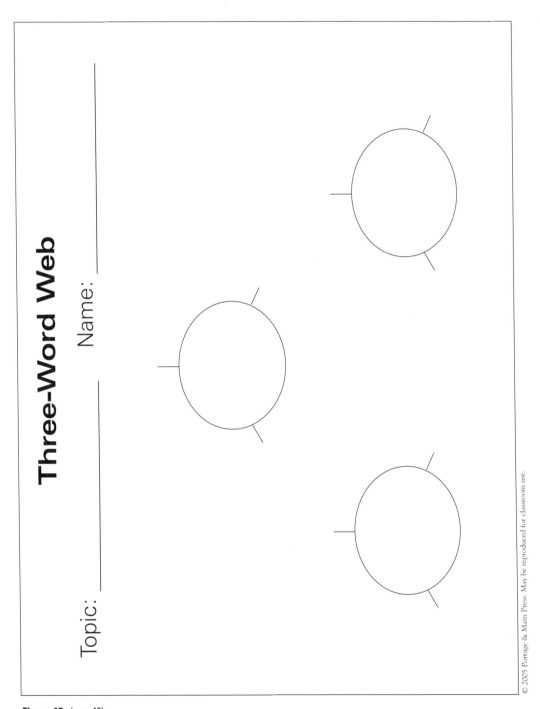

Figure 45. (page 43)

Teach-It Feedback

To: _____
   (teach-it group)

From: _____
   (peer)

I learned:

_____

_____

_____

I liked:

_____

_____

_____

Figure 49. (page 45)

Retelling Frame

My favourite is _____

5 – 7 KEY IDEAS	OBJECTS or SYMBOLS

Figure 51. (page 47)

1. "Thinking and talking about experiences not only helps make sense of the past but also changes the likelihood of subsequent remembering."
   — Daniel Schacter, *The Seven Sins of Memory*

2. "...simple acts of social caring can create positive affects for others."
   — Maja Storch, *Make Yourself Happy*

3. "Making choices is like lifting weights. The more frequently students choose from a group of options the thicker their 'responsibility muscles' become."
   — Thomas Armstrong, *Multiple Intelligence in the Classroom*

4. "...if students are able to vebalize and "flesh out" ideas with other students, or work together on group projects, the thought becomes anchored in understanding."
   — Carla Hannaford, *Smart Moves*

5. "...if the questions probe deeper for thoughtful answers,...then the response becomes more elaborate and the thinking is extended and deepened."
   — Robin Fogarty, *Brain Compatible Classrooms*

6. "... 'energizers' or quick little wake up activities increase energy levels, improve storage and recall of information, and help learners feel good."
   — Eric Jensen, *Learning With the Body in Mind*

7. "Novelty is an effective tool for maintaining student interest and engagement.... Student focus increases because the unexpected is happening."
   — David Sousa, *The Leadership Brain*

8. "When classroom teachers give (descriptive) feedback they create a climate of success."
   — Candace Pert, *Molecules of Emotion*

9. "Celebrating student learning is the most fundamental, most motivating and most powerful affirmation for the learning community."
   — Judy Carr and Douglas Harris, *Succeeding with Standards*

10. "Stronger memories are formed each time the information is expressed... even when the review is very brief."
    — Candace Pert, *Molecules of Emotion*

Brain Bits (page 50)

Planning Sheet   Name: _____

The section I'm focusing on is _____

_____

The idea I'm going to try is _____

_____

_____

Subject/topic/assignment I'm using it for is _____

_____

Time frame: by _____
                           (date of next meeting)

Comments:

What worked: _____

_____

_____

What didn't work: _____

_____

_____

Adaptations made: _____

_____

_____

Planning Sheet

Recording Sheet

Name: _____

Contents	Ideas Tried	Comments
RELATIONSHIPS Remember When Special Thanks Sign Up Leave Your Mark Keepers		
ORGANIZATION Contract Time Reading Roles Hands Down Brain Breaks Subject Marathon		
ASSESSMENT Peer Feedback Comments Only Class-Constructed Rubrics Wrap-Up Portfolios Portfolio Showing		
RELIABLES Questions and Clues Summary Frames Teach It Storytellers 60-Second Flashbacks		

Recording Sheet

Bibliography

Armstrong, Thomas. *Multiple Intelligences in the Classroom, 2nd Ed.* Alexandria, VA: Association for Supervision and Curriculum Development (ASCD), 2001.

Black, Paul, Christine Harison, Clare Lee, Bethan Marshall, Dylan Wiliam. *Assessment for Learning: Putting it into Practice.* Berkshire, UK: Open University Press, 2003.

Carr Judy, Douglas Harris. *Succeeding with Standards.* Alexandria, VA: Association for Supervision and Curriculum Development (ASCD), 2001.

Daniels, Harvey. *Literature Circles. Voice and Choice in Book Clubs and Reading Groups.* Portland, ME: Pembroke Publishers, 2002.

Fogarty, Robin. *Brain Compatible Classrooms, 2nd Ed.* Arlington Heights, IL: Skylight Professional Development, 1997.

Gregory, Kathleen, Caren Camreron, Anne Davies. *Knowing What Counts: Setting and Using Criteria.* Merville, BC: Connections Publishing, 1997.

Gregory, Kathleen, Caren Cameron, Anne Davies. *Knowing What Counts: Self-Assessment and Goal-Setting.* Merville, BC: Connections Publishing, 2000.

Gregory, Kathleen, Caren Cameron, Anne Davies. *Knowing What Counts: Conferencing and Reporting.* Merville, BC: Connections Publishing, 2001.

Hannaford, Carla. *Smart Moves: Why Learning Is Not All In Your Head.* Arlington, VA: Great Ocean Publishers, 1995.

Harmin, Merrill. *Inspiring Active Learning.* Alexandria, VA: Association for Supervision and Curriculum Development (ASCD), 1994.

Jensen, Eric. *Brain-Based Learning.* Del Mar, CA: The Brain Store, 2000.

Jensen, Eric. *Learning With the Body in Mind: The Scientific Basis for Energizers, Movement, Play, Games, and Physical Education.* San Diego: The Brain Store, 2000.

Levine M.D., Mel. *The Myth of Laziness.* New Yok, NY: Simon & Shuster, 2003.

Kaufeldt, Martha. *Begin With the Brain: Orchestrating the Learner-Centered Classroom.* Tuscon, AZ: Zephyr Press, 1999.

Markowitz, Karen, Eric Jansen. *Great Memory Book.* San Diego, CA: The Brain Store, 1999.

Pert, Candace. *Molecules of Emotion.* New York, NY: Scibner, 1997.

Schacter, Daniel. *The Seven Sins of Memory: How the Mind Forgets and Remembers.* Boston, MA: Houghton Mifflin, 2001.

Sousa, David A. *The Leadership Brain: How to Lead Today's Schools More Effectively.* Thousand Oaks, CA: Corwin Press, 2003.

Storch, Maja. "Think Better: Make Yourself Happy," *Scientific American Mind,* Vol. 16, No.1 (April, 2005).

Workshops

The authors are available to do workshops on the Voices of Experience series of books. If you enjoyed this book, you'll love their workshops!

Here's what participants are saying:

> "Brilliant. Thank you for giving me such wonderful ideas to take back to my class."

> "The ideas are easy, inexpensive, and require little preparation."

> "Great energy. Wonderful ideas that can be used immediately!"

> "Many of your ideas will show up in my class this week. Thanks, too, for the chuckles."

> "Thanks, I had fun. I learned a lot and my kids will benefit right away."

> "Your ideas help me do the best for my students and still have a life for myself."

For more information, please contact Portage & Main Press at 1-800-667-9673.